Inspirational
Silk Painting from Nature

RENATE HENGE

Edited by Pam Dawson

SEARCH PRESS, TUNBRIDGE WELLS, ENGLAND
in association with
MAX A. HARRELL, VICTORIA, AUSTRALIA

Contents

Introduction

We live in a wonderful natural world, full of colour, light and shade, shape and texture, which most of us either fail to see, or simply take for granted. In previous centuries man lived close to the soil and was aware of the changing seasons and the rhythm of life but today, society has become more and more remote from nature.

When we open a tin of convenience food, or heat up a pre-packaged meal, we are hardly aware of our dependency upon the earth's vegetation. Throughout the year we have a choice of exotic fruits and vegetables available from every part of the globe, but we no longer have any idea of the rigours involved in their planting and harvesting. We have become a society with everything we desire at our command yet, to counteract the stress of modern life, we yearn to be at one with our roots again.

The threat to the environment through the exploitation of its resources and the pollution of industry is now an accepted fact and the signs are visible wherever we look. More and more people are coming to realize that we must conserve nature and the first step must surely be a better understanding and appreciation of all we see around us. When we can enjoy looking at the beauty of a cloud formation; the shapes and textures of trees and animals; the changes in light and mood during a day, or discover the intricate structure of a rock, we are more than halfway there.

When our eyes are truly opened, we will perhaps feel impelled to capture what we see for our own satisfaction, or to give pleasure to others. We may wish to catch a moment in time exactly as it was, or change it to fit into a personal fantasy. As a way of expressing these feelings, some will want to explore traditional techniques such as watercolouring, or painting in oils, but more than any other medium, painting on silk can be used to represent the subtleties of nature. The lustre of the silk background adds sheen to the painting and the way in which the colours run into each other, and blend together, can create a magical effect.

The ancient technique of painting on silk came originally from China, the homeland of silk. It was rediscovered and developed in France early in the present century and very quickly became an established craft. Today it is becoming increasingly popular as an art form, as its full potential is realized. Happily, however, the technique need not be restricted to pictures alone, as it can be used to decorate clothing, such as shawls and scarves, or household items such as cushions and quilts, and has many other applications.

This book concentrates on the design of suitable motifs for silk painting. The individual preparation and assembly of specific articles, or the positioning of the motifs, is not dealt with and belongs in another book. It is intended to inspire you to interpret nature and use your own ideas, then apply them in whatever way you choose. It is hoped that beginners, as well as experienced painters will enjoy browsing through this book and discover a new way of capturing nature.

8

Finding the inspiration

When we are children we find it easy to paint and depict, with great imagination, the object or experience that has inspired us. A handle added to a square gives us an elephant trumpeting through the jungle; two bumps, a head and legs and a camel marches across the desert, while a large circle for a body and head, little legs and a beak easily describe a bird.

The especial charm of naive painting is this concentration on what is important and children have a distinct advantage here.They can often see beautiful or frightening images in inanimate objects such as cracks in a wall, fabric or wallpaper patterns, or reflections in a fire. Most of us have memories of scaring ourselves half to death with goblins and witches who only existed in our imagination! It is interesting to note that Paul Klee's first inspiration came from looking at marble-topped tables.

In later years we become critical of these early efforts and their amateurish execution embarrasses us. We no longer paint with conviction what we see and like, or what we personally want to express, but fall back on preconceived ideas and traditions. We buy the necessary materials with great enthusiasm and then either fail to find a subject to which we can relate or, if we do, lack the courage to begin. A bought kit, complete with instructions, can save us from complete failure but this is 'painting by numbers', and real pleasure only comes from our own creative ideas.

To create our own pictures we must first of all forget everything other people before us have painted. Ignore the wealth of material in our Art Galleries and books full of technical advice, at least for the time being. Instead, begin to explore for yourself the infinite range of colours, forms and textures to be found in nature. You will not need to go far to collect seeds, fruits, feathers, shells, roots and leaves, as well as many other normally unobserved objects. It is a good idea to take a camera or sketch book when you are out walking, to capture the effects of light and shade, or those items that cannot be taken away, such as wild flowers.

When you have collected sufficient items of interest, arrange them on a flat surface in a way that pleases you. Maybe the contrast in textures of a feather placed against a shell satisfies you, or muted colours juxtaposed against bright, bold ones stir your imagination. When you are sure the resulting arrangement is as you wish to see it, you are ready to begin painting on silk.

Try and capture the effect you see by applying pure, or mixed colours to a piece of silk. Half close your eyes so that the items merge into each other or, better still, listen to some music that will enable you to lose yourself, so that your movements are no longer deliberate and self-conscious. Try adding some wax or gutta lines, not to confine shapes but in a completely random way.

Stop every so often to view what you have in front of you. Your picture may just be an abstract harmony of colours but as you look at it, your inner eye may conjure up something new and exciting. Don't be afraid to turn the painting upside down to see the effect. Sometimes the way in which the colour has already been applied will give a certain impression. For instance, if it has been painted in horizontal lines, landscapes instantly spring to mind, maybe one you have actually seen, or one imagined.

You can enhance your picture with the addition of suitable spirit, or water, once it is dry, or by sprinkling salt on the fabric while it is still wet. The spirit, or water, will push the colours away from each other, and where salt comes into contact with the paint, it will concentrate the colours.

Water can be used to produce structures which remind us of forests, mountains or waves. Dabbed on spots of spirit or water can give the appearance of stones, puddles, trees or blossom. Experiment to see what effects you can achieve. For instance, the bleakness of a landscape can be softened with the addition of a tree; a blossom can be defined with the addition of a stamen and pistil; movement in water can be suggested with a few swaying reeds, or a stone made to appear porous with a few fine droplets of spirit.

Coarse salt sprinkled over the painted silk while it is still wet will produce feathery effects and if you apply colour to silk that has been impregnated with salt, the resulting pattern will resemble coral. Yet another effect can be achieved by softly blowing wet paint over silk which has been treated with a foundation in a mixture of gutta and spirit.

The more you experiment the more you will see that the different techniques used in silk painting produce spontaneous shapes and patterns which often remind you of natural images. It is not necessary to complete a painting at one sitting, in fact, if you put your work aside and come back to it you will often see some aspect which you had previously missed. Perhaps when you are in a different mood, or you look at it in a different light, it will become a source of inspiration.

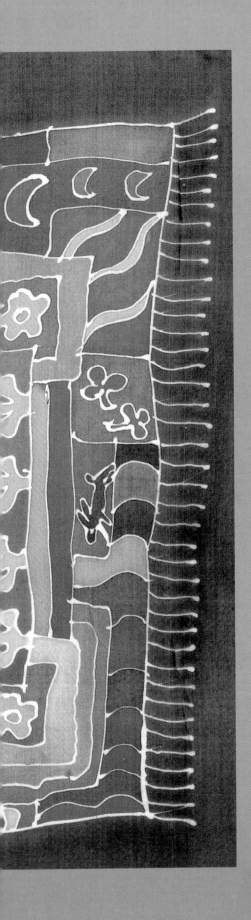

The art of painting on silk

Tools and materials

Silk

Most varieties of silk make suitable backgrounds for painting but to begin with, do not choose a fabric which is too thick. All kinds of what are termed 'pongé' silks, as well as crepe de chine, satin and twill, are perfect for silk pictures. Cheaper, very fine pongé silk is not to be recommended, however, as the pins used to stretch the silk can easily make holes in the fabric. Also, such fine silk is liable to be damaged by the spirit used for removing the gutta.

For blouses, dresses, jackets, scarves, shawls and cushions, crease-resistant crepe de chine is ideal, as well as shiny satin, strong twill and Habutai or Hanon silk. Soft, gossamer-like shawls can be made from chiffon or georgette.

Before beginning to paint, always check to see if the silk has been treated with a dressing. If a drop of paint does not spread quickly on the silk, the dressing has to be washed out of the fabric before you can begin to paint. Wild silk, and heavier types of silk should always be washed first, especially when they are being used for clothing, as they may shrink when being laundered.

Paints

Because of the enormous popularity of painting on silk, not only for pictures but also for clothing, new paints resistant to washing and dry cleaning were produced by the manufacturers. When items have to be laundered, the colours must stay luminous and clear, even after frequent washing or cleaning.

These paints have to be 'fixed' when the painting is completed, either by ironing, with chemicals or by steaming. Do check which method is to be used according to the manufacturer's instructions. They can also be thinned down with water or alcohol, (or a cheaper type of spirit such as lighter fuel) and if they are left in a dark place and kept tightly closed, they should last for years.

The easiest paints to use are those which are fixed by the ironing method, as apart from the iron, no other tools are needed. Unfortunately, these are not suitable for all silk painting techniques, and effects created with water and alcohol may not always be satisfactory.

Chemical reactive paints can be purchased together with the appropriate fixing fluid. This is brushed on to the dry painting and after an hour or so, it is washed out. However, if the fixing fluid is unevenly applied, or is too thin, then the paints will bleed into each other, or wash out. It is therefore best to apply the fixing fluid to both sides of the painting, especially when using thicker fabrics.

Steam-fixed paints are readily available and are used by most professional silk painters. However, even after fixing these colours as recommended by the manufacturer, they cannot be guaranteed absolutely colourfast.

Whether the paints have been fixed in a steamer, or by other means, the gutta can be washed out if it is water-soluble, otherwise remove with spirit. Surplus paint is often removed by both methods.

Many craft shops operate a 'fixing service', using special apparatus, but they will usually only accept large pieces. This equipment is available to any painter but is only economical if it is to be used regularly.

Gutta

The effect of gutta, or resist, in silk painting is similar to that produced by wax in batik techniques. Where the gutta is applied, the paint is prevented from penetrating the fabric and the flow of the paint is controlled. Areas of different colour can therefore be kept separate and shape contours can also be drawn. Spirit or water-soluble gutta can be obtained and with the help of a special dispenser, the clear, syrupy fluid can be applied to the silk in fairly fine lines. Water-soluble gutta can also be coloured with the addition of a little silk paint.

With both types of gutta, very fine lines have a tendency to break, allowing the paint to seep through, but if you apply it in rather thick lines, the outlines are quite prominent when the gutta has been washed out. Great care should be taken to ensure that the gutta is completely dry before beginning to paint.

The consistency of the gutta must be adjusted to the type of silk being used. Thicker silk requires thinner gutta, so that it can penetrate the fabric more easily. Thin the gutta as recommended by the manufacturer and test it on a small piece of silk first. It is also advisable to check the completed gutta outlines of a design against the light, so that any break, or lines which are too thin, can be seen and corrected.

Wax

Beeswax and candle wax can be used as a resist, instead of gutta, for silk painting. The wax has to be heated in a saucepan first, taking care not to have it too hot, or it will damage the silk. Test it by letting a spot of wax drop on to the silk. If the wax looks grey it has penetrated the silk, if it stays white it is not hot enough.

Beeswax is very pliable and suitable for fine designs, while the harder candle wax breaks easily and is therefore ideal for 'cracked' effects. To achieve this, scrunch the waxed surface and paint over the lines, so that coloured hair-lines appear along the cracks.

Wax can be applied with a tjan, used for batik, or with a variety of shaped brushes. Before fixing the paints, the wax must be removed by ironing.

Frames

During painting, the silk has to be fully suspended and must not touch any surface. Pieces of silk which have already been cut and shaped, or finished garments, are difficult to paint and it is better to work with an obling or square piece of silk, so that it is really taut when fixed to the frame.

To stretch the silk use drawing pins or, preferably, three-pronged pins and push them into the frame at intervals of about 4–5cm (1½–2in). The wood used for the frame must be soft enough to take the pins but strong enough not to give under tension. Before beginning any project, cover the frame with adhesive tape. It can then be easily wiped clean and remains of paint from previous work will not spoil a new piece of silk.

If a large area of silk is being painted, the wet silk will sag in the middle and you must ensure that it does not touch the surface on which the frame is placed. If necessary lift the frame on to some wooden blocks and re-adjust the tension of the silk.

If very straight lines are included in a design, the background colour has to be applied first, dried thoroughly and then the silk is removed from the frame. The silk will not distort or stretch much further now and can be placed in the frame again and held by adhesive tape, with just a few pins for extra security. The lines will now be absolutely straight, especially if drawn with a ruler.

Brushes

It is a false economy to buy cheap brushes for painting on silk. You should choose the best hair brush available, clean it well after every painting session and never leave the bristles standing in water. A thick brush of good quality will keep its shape and give you pleasure for many years.

A thick brush holds a lot of paint and releases it very slowly, so it is useful for painting fine detail, as well as for colouring in large areas. In addition, you will need some stiff brushes of varying widths, useful for applying a lighter tone on top of a dark one.

You must work quickly and to cover large surfaces use foam brushes. Remember to have a fine brush handy for filling in any nooks or crannies you may have missed. See to it that the surface remains wet. Where there is a central design, paint alternatively on both sides of this, so as to keep both sides wet.

Other materials and tools

Most of the additional requirements will be found among ordinary household items. These include beakers for water, spirit and paints; screw-top jars for mixing colours and storing leftovers; swabs of cotton wool held with a clothes peg for painting large areas; cotton wool buds for bleaching out colour with spirit. You will also need cellotape, scissors, a ruler, pencils, drawing pins or three-pronged tacks, rubber gloves and maybe an apron. Extra items may be required such as lighter fuel, coarse salt, a hair dryer, and a pen nib to fix to a gutta dispenser for very fine lines.

When the painting is completely dry, depending on the method of fixing you use, you may also need tissue paper, newspapers at least six weeks old, aluminium foil, an electric iron, a hotplate or hob, and a cooking pot with a sieve and separate water container, or a pressure cooker.

Crown of a tree in salt technique.

Prominent white contours achieved with white gutta, right.

Handling the materials

Mixing the paint

The paints available for silk painting are highly concentrated, so they have to be thinned down to a greater or lesser degree before use. Most products can be thinned with water, or alcohol, which changes the viscosity of the paint. Silk paints which have been applied undiluted often bleed, or wash out, when rinsed after fixing, as the surplus paint not taken up by the fabric lifts off.

Thinning with colourless alcohol, or cheaper lighter fuel, encourages the penetration of the paint into the fabric. For instance, red slightly diluted with alcohol will look more brilliant after fixing than red applied undiluted.

When a large area is to be painted it is not advisable to use alcohol on its own as a thinner. Neither is it recommended that water is used on its own, as paints diluted with water do not spread very freely and the colouring becomes a little irregular. Water evaporates more slowly than alcohol, so a mixture of half water and half alcohol makes it possible to paint evenly and at a slower pace.

When working on a smaller scale, you must consider the techniques to be used, before deciding on the preparation of the paints. Mixing with alcohol means the paint dries quickly, while water, or a mixture of water and alcohol, calls for a longer drying time.

Applying the paint

Paints can be applied either with a brush, cotton wool or an air brush. While most fabric paints stick to the surface of the fabric and look dull, silk paints penetrate the fibres completely and spread and shimmer to give a brilliant effect. Provided the silk has not been impregnated first, see page 17, the wetter the paint is applied, the more it will spread.

Try the following experiments to see the effects you can create. Paint dripped on to dry silk and left to dry will create an area of colour with a dark rim. Especially strong lines appear where two different colours flow towards each other. On silk previously dampened with water, the colours will flow into each other and will dry without a rim. During this process, it sometimes happens that the mixed colours separate out into their original components.

Colour changes

An area painted with soft colours looks more artistic and interesting than one painted in one colour or tone only.

Soft colour changes are best achieved on a damp background. The paints to be used are mixed with approximately equal parts water and alcohol, and applied with bold strokes. While still wet, they are rubbed into each other vigorously until no harsh contrasts, or lines, are visible. To make the transition between contrasting colours easier, add one or two tones of each colour in between.

To paint large areas, well soaked but not dripping wet cotton wool swabs of paint are useful. Hold them with a clothes peg, or tie them on to a small stick. Smaller areas are painted with a soft brush, then a stiff brush rubbed over the changes.

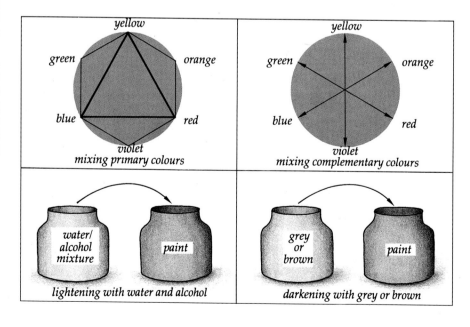

mixing primary colours

mixing complementary colours

lightening with water and alcohol

darkening with grey or brown

Mixing colours and tones

For the beginner the mixing of colours often creates the most problems, but just by using the three primary colours, yellow, red and blue, (which cannot be produced by mixing other colours), you can achieve any number of different shades. When two out of these three colours are mixed together, you create either orange, green or violet. As yellow pigments are not as strong as red or blue, when mixing them you need at least twice as much yellow to red or blue. Always begin with the lightest colour and add the darker ones drop by drop, using a small eye dropper kept for this purpose and cleaned after each use, otherwise you waste too much paint. An arrangement of related colour shades, called a colour wheel, can be made showing smaller and smaller colour differences, until the eye finds it very difficult to detect any division.

All of these are pure, brilliant colours, composed of no more than two primary colours. Duller, cloudy colours are achieved by mixing all three primary colours, or when a pure colour is mixed with its complementary colour, shown opposite it on the colour circle. For instance, a dark grey is produced when pure yellow, red and blue are mixed in equal parts. If you want a dull green, just add a little red, the complementary colour to green.

To have as many colours as possible available, you can mix pure colours and duller versions by adding their complementary colours, and you can also create lighter and darker tones of each colour. To lighten a colour you add a mixture of water and alcohol in equal parts, drop by drop until you achieve the

tone you require. To darken a colour, add either brown made up of seven parts yellow, three parts red and two parts blue, or grey made up of yellow, red and blue in equal parts. Black paint is also available but this should be used very sparingly.

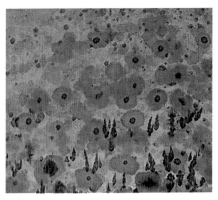

The scarf at the top has yellow, brown earthy colours enriched with brilliant complementary colours.

Only the softness of the lines was of interest in this quieter 'wood-grain' effect.

A poppy field with warm colours splashed on was enlivened with the addition of light and dark green details.

Thinning with alcohol and water

Lightening the tone of a specific area after it has been painted and allowed to dry can add another dimension to a painting. Alcohol and water can be used to achieve these effects. The colour pigment is only displaced and will settle somewhere else in higher density, creating most interesting designs.

Pigments displaced with alcohol appear especially bright and clear. With a cotton wool swab, or brush, dipped in colourless alcohol, a line or area is 'washed out'. The rubbed off colour settles and dries as a dark rim. A repetition of this process strengthens the effect, but the silk must be allowed to dry to the touch between applications. Colour displacement on a wet ground only spreads out again and after a short time, the effect is lost. However, paintings which have been allowed to dry for days are very difficult to lighten in this way, as the paints are already bonded to the silk.

Lightened areas with dark rims can be created in a more controlled way with the help of a hair dryer, as alcohol lines 'freeze' immediately when moisture is removed. When the line has reached a pleasing shape and you do not want it to move any further, simply stop it with the dryer. Do note that too high a temperature may result in uneven drying of the paint, or may even damage the silk.

Lightening a colour with water may also add interest to an otherwise monotone area. These colour displacements are not as strong as those achieved with alcohol but the rim lines turn out darker. To achieve very dark lines plenty of water must be applied and it must be allowed to dry naturally. A hair dryer is not advisable in this case. This technique only works on a dry background.

Salt effects

Colour displacement with salt is one of the most popular techniques for an inexperienced silk painter. In a few minutes, as though drawn by an invisible hand, surprising patterns appear on the damp silk as the salt attracts the moisture. The application of fine or coarse salt allows small areas of the wet painting to be drained of colour, and the pigment is collected in dark lines or dots around the grains of salt. Lightened areas appear, which may be round or elongated.

The painted area has to be damp, but not wet when the salt is applied or the salt grains will 'drown'. The salt must also be very dry and it is as well to dry it in an oven first. To give the salt enough time to be active, thin the paint down with water and work in a room which is not too warm.

Another effect is achieved when you sprinkle salt on to a wet background and then apply the paint around it. In this case, the paint streaks will move outwards away from the salt. Should the brush come into contact with any of the salt it must be washed out thoroughly, as any salt in the paint will contaminate it.

With both these effects, when the painting is completely dry, the salt can be shaken or brushed off, or it will leave unwanted blotches behind. Salt techniques can liven up a painting but they should never be used to excess.

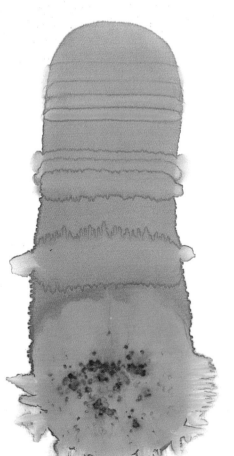

Lightening with alcohol in 4 steps.

} 1   } 2   } 3   } 4   steps

Lightening with water stopped with a hair dryer.

} 1   } 2   } 3   steps

Lightening with water, allowed to spread and evaporate slowly.

Coarse salt was sprinkled on to the damp silk. The moisture creeps towards the salt in the centre and carries colour pigments with it, which accumulate near the salt whilst the surrounding areas become lighter in tone.

Impregnations

If you want to work without gutta, or a resist, but still don't want the colours to run into each other, the silk can be impregnated before applying the paint. There are a number of ways to restrict the fluidity of the paint, so that the painting of even very fine lines is possible.

Paints applied to wet silk and next to each other will run like water colours. To stop this, dry areas need to be glazed over. A special anti-fusant is available and you can paint on silk treated with this mixture just as you would on paper. You can also apply many of the techniques used on paper, such as spraying, sponging, ragging or blowing. For these methods the paint should be thinned down with alcohol to avoid 'beading'.

You can also apply a film of wax, which has been ironed into the silk by placing it between sheets of clean paper. When the wax has hardened, lively coloured areas can be created with bold brush strokes.

Silk can also be impregnated with a solution of salt, made from about 250g (9oz) of kitchen salt to 1lt (1¾pt) of warm water. Silk impregnated with this solution can take on a number of characteristics. With a strong impregnation of several applications, allowed to dry slowly, large salt crystals show as dots. If paint is dabbed on to the silk, it will branch out like coral, creating many interesting structures.

If the silk is dipped into the solution, squeezed out and dried quickly, the salt crystal will be finely distributed, so that soft painted effects are possible. Especially effective patterns are created by this method when alcohol is applied to otherwise plain coloured areas.

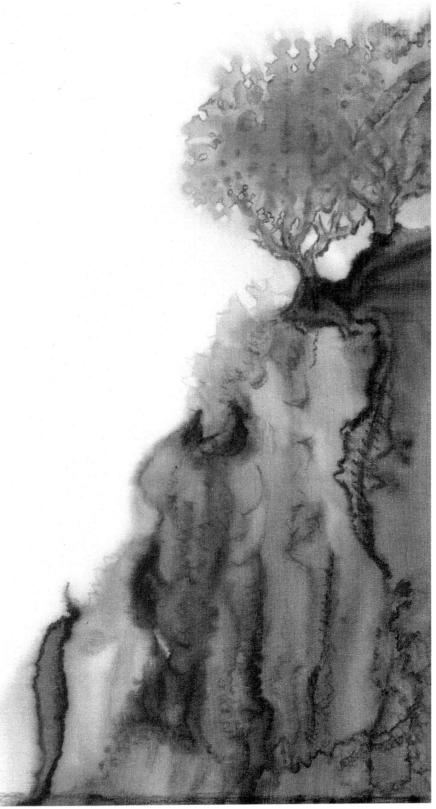

A rocky coast painted on to silk impregnated with a salt solution.

Painting with wax

Batik, from Asia, is an ancient way of dyeing fabric. With this technique selected areas are covered with hot wax, for instance, the outline of a motif. When the silk is dipped into a dye bath, the dye cannot penetrate these waxed areas. Multicoloured designs are created when, after the first dye bath, the dried fabric is covered with more wax and dipped again into a bath of different coloured dye. Cracks in the wax can cause the appearance of fine coloured veins, known as the 'crackle' effect.

This technique is also possible with silk paints, but the tedious dipping and washing becomes superfluous as the stretched silk can be painted with cotton wool swabs, or a large brush. Different colours can be used to paint the areas separated by the wax. The crackle effect of the batik technique can be simulated by covering the whole, or part of the painting with hot wax. When the wax has dried, scrunch it up and then paint over the cracked wax. This technique is known as 'false batik'.

If you experiment with this batik technique you will be able to create all kinds of effects. A line drawn with a brush dipped in wax is often livlier than a line of gutta. Using a comb like a broad brush, parallel lines can be produced and astonishing results can be achieved with spots and splashes of wax.

The use of gutta, or resist

If the painting is to incorporate the use of gutta, or a resist, you must begin with a well thought-out design, as it is impossible to change anything once the gutta has been applied.

To make sure the design outlines are correct, it is best to first draw them to their original size on paper, using Indian ink or a felt-tipped pen. Then the fabric to be painted is stretched over the drawing, fixed with adhesive tape and the design lines copied with a soft pencil. Thicker fabric can be attached to a window with adhesive tape, with the design behind it so that it can be seen through the fabric.

While outlining with gutta you must make sure that no unwanted drops fall on to the stretched silk. It helps to practise on paper first. Hold the dispenser like a pen and gently squeeze out the gutta through the fine nozzle. For very fine lines a gutta pen is used. The first drop of gutta should be wiped off the nozzle with some paper, also make sure there are no air bubbles. The long, even pressure on the dispenser is a matter of practice.

To make sure that all the gutta lines are unbroken, hold the silk up to the light, and repair any breaks. Now let the gutta drain back from the nozzle into the dispenser before closing it, so that the opening does not become clogged up. Thin gutta lines dry quickly, so you can soon begin painting with the lightest tones first. Should it happen that a gutta line is broken and paint escapes, you can repair the line after the paint is dry. Lighten the error with alcohol and then apply a darker tone. The mistake will hardly be noticeable.

As silk paint runs as soon as it comes into contact with the fabric, it is best to keep the brush away from

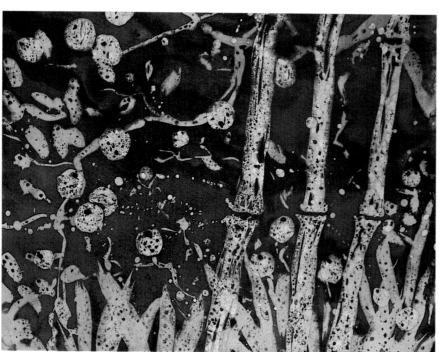

Above, the wax was brushed and splashed on. If the fabric is scrunched up before painting, fine 'veins' will appear where the wax has cracked.

Paint the outlines on to light coloured silk with wax, then work over it with darker silk paints. When repeated several times, interesting mixed tones will appear.

the gutta lines. Also make sure surplus paint is wiped off the brush, to avoid any drips. You should work briskly from one side to the other to avoid patchy, dried out rims.

Gutta lines applied to white silk will remain white after the painting has been fixed and washed. These are in keeping when other white, or light areas are included in the design. If you want to avoid white lines and don't wish to use coloured gutta, you can dip the silk into dye before you begin to paint and allow it to dry.

Fixing the paints

If the colours on unfixed silk paintings are exposed to sunlight they will be bleached out within a few days. They are also easily affected by dampness. To make the paints colourfast, they have to be fixed. Depending on the manufacturer's instructions, some paints can be fixed with an iron, others with chemicals, or steamed in a steamer or pressure cooker. The first two methods are very simple but the steaming method is more difficult.

To steam fix a painting allow the silk to dry for at least 12 hours. So that no discolouration or staining occurs, it is important that the silk does not come into contact with any water and that it is only penetrated by the steam. To achieve this, roll the silk between double layers of six weeks old newspapers, or kitchen towelling, making sure there are no creases in the silk and that the paper overlaps on both sides by at least 5cm (2in), Fig a. Seal with adhesive tape, Fig b. Line a sieve or tray with newspaper and fit in the rolled up parcel, Fig c.

Put 2cm (¾in) of water into the steamer, add the sieve with the silk parcel and elevate it on an upside down cup or dish, to make sure that no water can reach the silk. Cover the sieve with a dome of aluminium foil to stop any drips of condensation falling on to the silk. The steaming process in a pressure cooker will take about 45 minutes at mark 2. Without pressure it will take at least twice as long.

The fixed silk painting should be rinsed in plenty of cold water, to which a dash of vinegar has been added, Fig e, then ironed whilst still damp, Fig. f. Avoid soaking in water for any length of time, as well as scrunching up, as some bleeding of surplus colours can be expected. The silk can be patted dry with a clean cloth. Gutta lines which are not soluble in water are removed with dry-cleaning liquid before washing the silk. Gold and silver gutta should also be dry-cleaned.

When you use a commercial steamer do not roll the silk up too tightly, to allow the steam to penetrate the silk. The outermost layer of paper can be protected against condensation by a layer of aluminium foil, provided sufficient steam can enter from the base.

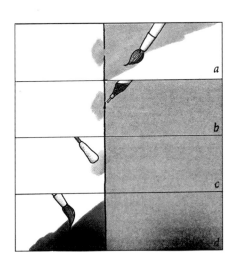

A leak in the resist line is mended, the paint bleached with alcohol and painted over with a darker colour.

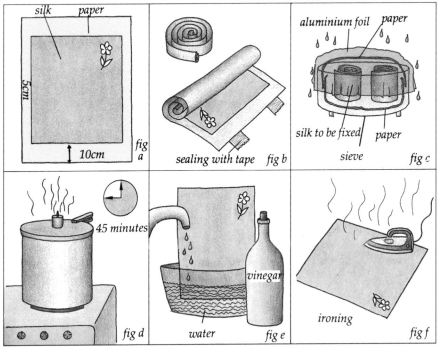

Designing from nature

Design criterions

Composition

Of course it is impossible to give you exact composition rules here, which would turn each one of your creations into a masterpiece, but it is possible to help you shake off some of your uncertainty. Children paint with confidence, balancing form and colour instinctively and organizing shapes according to their importance. As adults, we have to think about the composition of a picture. Once we find a motif we would like to paint on silk, we first have to make sure that it has the right proportions for the area of silk. The frame will eventually limit the space into which we have to fit all the important components of the picture.

To depict the chosen subject accurately, first look at its shape. Even the most complicated forms can be simplified and broken down into a few, more basic shapes. In the two-dimensional world of painting, these would include circles, rectangles and triangles. Something as complex as the body of an animal, the branch of a tree or a blossom can be drawn with such simple shapes. The necessary details, such as light, shadow, pattern and structure can be added later.

Generally, when painting we make the image we have chosen smaller than life-size. We also turn a three-dimensional structure into a two-dimensional picture. For this to be successful, it is essential to understand the proper relationship of the proportions of the subject. We must decide how the length and breadth of a specific shape relate to each other, also to the other subjects in the picture. Begin by sketching out ideas on paper until you have put the picture together. In this instance it must be a case of

everyone in their own fashion! Some may start work on the silk straight away; others may want to experiment with more sketches, or cut out some of the shapes so that they can be arranged to find the most pleasing composition.

One single object, placed as a motif in the middle of the silk will already make a picture. Even here, however, we have interesting possibilities which will produce different effects. Just by moving this object out of the centre, the overall balance is broken. If it is so large that it fills the whole picture, or we just show part of it, this object may dominate, or even threaten, the composition. If it is so small that it appears to float in space, the effect will be quite different. You may wish to let the object enter the picture from one side, or even grow out of the side. You should certainly explore all these possibilities.

The background surrounding the object has shape and is also important to the final effect. Many shapes of equal size placed next to each other in an orderly row can radiate a feeling of calm and harmony, but the regularity of the items and the compensating background can appear dull. The most extreme example of this would be a painting

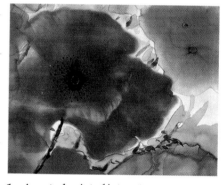

1. A central point of interest.

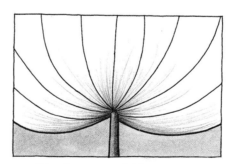

2. Filling the space available.

3. Uninteresting order.

4. Small shapes in a large space.

5. Three-dimensional variety.

22

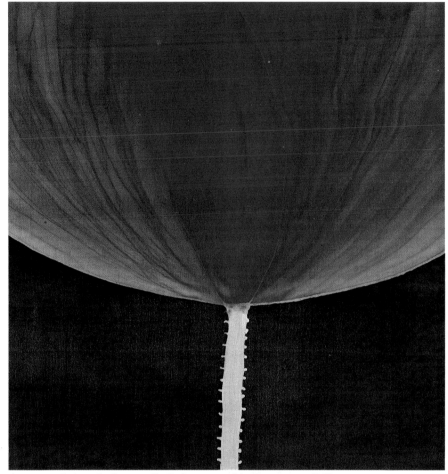

An unusual view of a flower, effectively arranged in the space available.

of a chess board, which expresses complete order with all the squares of equal importance. By contrast, a rhythmically divided composition, constructed of different shapes and sizes in irregular order, ensures that the eye keeps on finding something new.

Contrasts

Different shapes influence each other and their attraction, or repulsion, creates 'tension'. A painting without this element of tension is like an egg without salt and when it is lacking, a picture does not 'speak' to us. In a play, book or film, tension can develop with time but in a picture it has to be created immediately, with the help of contrasts in colour and shape.

The essential elements of a picture often appear to the viewer to be swinging between two poles; light and shade; large and small; sharp and round; straight and curved; near and far, and so on. These contrasts prevent too strict an order, making the painting more exciting. All these aspects of a painting have to be fitted into a pleasing composition and, in spite of their tension, have to create a harmonious whole.

In the beginning, it will seem difficult to change the unstructured, lifeless silk background into a lively, optical event. However, you will soon find it easy to recognize a spoiled composition and just a little willingness to experiment and plenty of patience will help you find your own style.

Straight/round.

Large/small.

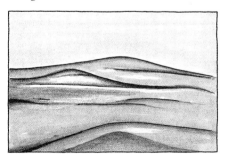

Light/dark.

Many/few.

23

Applied embellishments

Even in prehistoric times, everyday articles were embellished with decorations. This form of applied art has a role to play in silk painting. Items of clothing, such as blouses, household linen such as cushions, and accessories such as bags or brooches, become unique when decorated with silk painted motifs. It is interesting to note that, as in ancient times, natural forms are the best design source.

To design embellishments of this kind the characteristics of the natural subject must be retained, for example, the shape of the leaves of a flower and its silhouette. It is up

to you how far you want to simplify, or stylize the details. Geometric shapes can form the 'bricks' from which an animal or plant is built, so experiment with circles, curves, pentagons and hexagons. The chosen subject can be featured as a border, scattered over a background, repeated rhythmically horizontally, vertically, diagonally, or at random in any direction. However, it must always colour complement the item to which it is being applied and fit into the overall effect.

Embellishments of this kind often have a symbolic connotation, so you need not stick to the everyday items you see around you. Let your imagination run riot with mythological creatures, such as dragons and unicorns, and exotic plants from far away shores.

Opposite, a background of overlapping scale shapes can be highlighted with a motif taking a similar theme from nature.

These sketches show ways of placing the motifs.

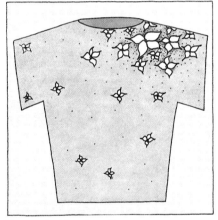

Scattered with point of interest.

T-shirt with a single motif.

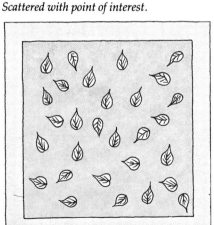

Motifs scattered on a scarf.

Central motif on a scarf.

Scarf with prominent border.

Colour composition

According to the artist, Georges Seurat, 'Art is harmony and harmony is the unity of contrasts and similarity in tone, colour and line'. This sums up the points already made that a picture is attractive to the eye when the shapes are well balanced and, as with a musical composition, the tones blend together to strike a pleasing chord.

Colour is a very personal perception, which is triggered off by visible light of a certain wavelength falling on to the retina of the eye and then being interpreted by the brain. Colours influence each other and the same shade of yellow can look brilliant or subtle, soft or bright, or dynamic and aggressive when placed against a dark, pale, or hot or cold-coloured background. This changeability is more vividly perceived when using strongly opposing colours, such as blue and orange, yellow and violet, red and green, as well as black and white.

Colours are known to affect our senses and we connect yellow and orange tones with warmth and fire, but blue strikes us as cold. Some colours, however, are difficult to categorize as warm or cold. Reds and greens, for instance, can be either warm or cold according to the proportion of yellow they contain and the background colour. In advertising, and many other fields of industry, the effect of colour is continuously analysed. Certain colours are known to activate and stimulate aggression, while others can bring feelings of happiness, calmness or sadness. These reactions are being used to create harmonious surroundings in factories and offices, to promote staff well-being with the result that less time is being lost for sickness.

As already stated, primary colours cannot be created from any others, but by mixing two primary colours you can produce almost limitless tones which flow into each other with hardly any perceptible change. In addition, these colours can be lightened to almost white, or darkened to verge on black. Softened, slightly greyish tones, however, are often more appealing than pure bright colours and when observing nature you will find that unadulterated brilliant colours are much rarer than you would imagine. To achieve this misty effect, try mixing complementary colours. For instance, a green created from blue and yellow can be made warmer by adding some red, or a mixture of blue and red made cooler by adding some yellow.

All mixed colours based on one primary colour belong to the same colour family. Try, for instance, to mix as many related yellows as possible or, by adding more blue, create stronger nuances of green. Gold and orange are produced when red is added to yellow, while adding the complementary colour violet to the family of yellow tones will create ochre and olive green. Do be careful, as one drop of another colour may already be too much! It is best to use a thinned down colour for mixing.

Colours which are related, such as yellow and orange, are harmonious but do not create the necessary tension. This is only attained when colours are introduced which contain none, or very little, of the main colour. Too many unrelated colours, however, will produce a motley effect and introduce an unwanted feeling of restlessness. Try working with two complementary colours, one of which will be dominant and present in many different tones, such as the family of yellow. A small area in the complementary colour, lilac, will be enough to strengthen the colour scheme and create excitement.

This panel shows how warm and cold colours can be interchanged and how opposing shapes add to the composition.

Another possibility is to play the light and dark effects of one colour against each other. In this instance, the actual colour value becomes secondary to the tone value. The effect of contrasting cold and warm colours is very useful in composition, where the dominant colours are those within the red and yellow range, or those within the blue spectrum. Colours shown opposite each other on the circle will give the necessary emphasis. The contrast between pure and duller mixed colours can also add interest to a painting.

Skilfully applied colour contrasts create excitement in a picture and also depth. The illusion of depth will already have been achieved by overlapping objects in graded sizes, but colour underlines this impression. Warm colours push into the foreground, while green, blue and violet tones recede into the distance. The distribution of light and shade is also important and helps to create space. Objects in the distance appear softer, less distinct and lighter in colour, because of the volume of air between them and the

beholder. By contrast, colours in the foreground appear darker and more intensive, while outlines, structures and patterns are more distinct.

A colour scheme has previously been likened to music and as the notes combine to form a melody, so colours should come together to produce a lively effect, with repetitions and contrasts. Music can be loud or soft, vigorous or dreamlike and colours should be used to

produce the same sensations. Finding the way to handle colours which most appeal to you, however, takes time and the old proverb, 'Practice makes perfect', must apply. In fact, colour composition can become an obsession, whether in fine art, photography or textile techniques but one that gives enormous satisfaction.

This page shows examples of colour contrasts.

Yellow tulips illustrate light and dark contrasts, underlined by green.

These fruits shine with many related colours, from green, yellow and orange to red.

An abstract cornfield painted in the yellow colour family, extended to green and brown.

Finding and translating designs

The search

Having discovered something about the use of materials and the laws of design in the previous chapters, you now need to obtain some practical experience. The first question to ask yourself is which object, or theme, shall I depict? The only answer is to cut yourself loose from old ideas and go in search of your own style!

You will find design sources everywhere in nature, large and dynamic or small and delicate. The swell of the ocean after a storm; the sunset; an opening blossom; a butterfly, or even dead leaves and garden pests. Beauty can be found even in the most insignificant things.

Anything which arouses our curiosity, our compassion or our anger can be the basis of a design. It is our individual approach to the subject which is of consequence. Our feelings towards a mountain we have climbed with great effort will differ from one seen on a postcard. The more our senses are involved in the composition of a painting, the more expressive the results. We must experience the softness of an animal's fur, the rough structure of a stone, or the slipperiness of ice before we can communicate this to the beholder.

The final picture

From the rich source of possibilities available, let us imagine that you have chosen a sunlit landscape as your subject. In the foreground you can see lush vegetation, in the middle distance a village and in the background, mountains and sky. Perhaps you have already taken a colour slide of a suitable scene while on holiday. You could enlarge and project this slide on to a piece of silk and trace over all the outlines. Perhaps a suitable illustration is available and if you trace a grid over this, it can be reduced or enlarged to any size on graph paper and then filled in freehand. In both instances the result would be a fairly faithful reproduction but one lacking in originality or any feeling of spontaneity.

To use a photographic copy of

This photograph shows the landscape which was reproduced as a silk painting, on the opposite page.

On the left you can see another interpretation of the theme, landscape with poppies. The inspiration here came from a slope crowned with poppies. The half-covered house in the distance creates depth.

any subject is seldom satisfying to the creative painter. The camera takes in everything, whether it is important or not, but when you are painting from what you see first-hand, you can make decisions on what to include or discard. Only the very experienced photographer will have the patience and skill to achieve harmony in a composition, ignoring some of the abundance of nature around him. However, you can make use of certain areas, or impressions in a photograph by superimposing cut-out mounts of varying sizes over the print.

Once you have selected a subject which gives you satisfaction, it is important to establish the centre point of your picture and move the proportions of the other components around it. Then draw a simple sketch. The distances and perspective of important points can be measured with a pencil held in the fingers of an outstretched hand. Once these proportions are sketched

in, the details can be added later. Check the sketch again to make sure that the balance is correct and that you have managed to express the necessary feeling of tension.

Before you begin to paint you must decide which technique you wish to use and what colour scheme will best enhance the subject. Do you want the colours to run into each other, as in a watercolour painting, or do you prefer the exact contours achieved with gutta outlines? Is the colour mood to be one of tranquility, or will it be vibrantly exciting? A painting containing too many different techniques and colour changes can become restless and confusing.

Don't be discouraged by the examples shown in this book. Begin with a small format, or a single motif. If something goes wrong a small piece of silk and a little paint can easily be replaced. Don't throw anything away, however, but examine the details of the spoilt work

carefully to try and see where you have gone wrong. In any event, you have gained invaluable experience which will benefit your future work and remember, we all make mistakes!

Carefully transfer the sketch to the silk and begin to paint. Work from the lighter background to the foreground. The outlines are defined with gutta. Make sure the colour tones are pleasing and don't try to use too many different techniques. Strong colour details can be added at the end.

When sketching pay attention to the correct proportions, especially vertical. At this preparatory stage, the shapes only need to be drawn in a simplified form and to add too much detail would only confuse. You can then decide which part of the picture you want to reproduce, checking the balance and tension of your composition.

The finished picture.

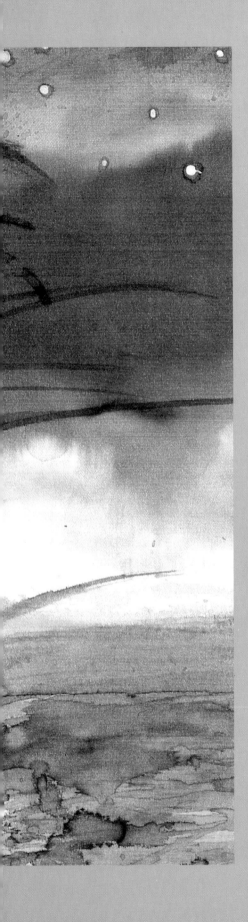

Motifs from nature

Rocks, stones and earth

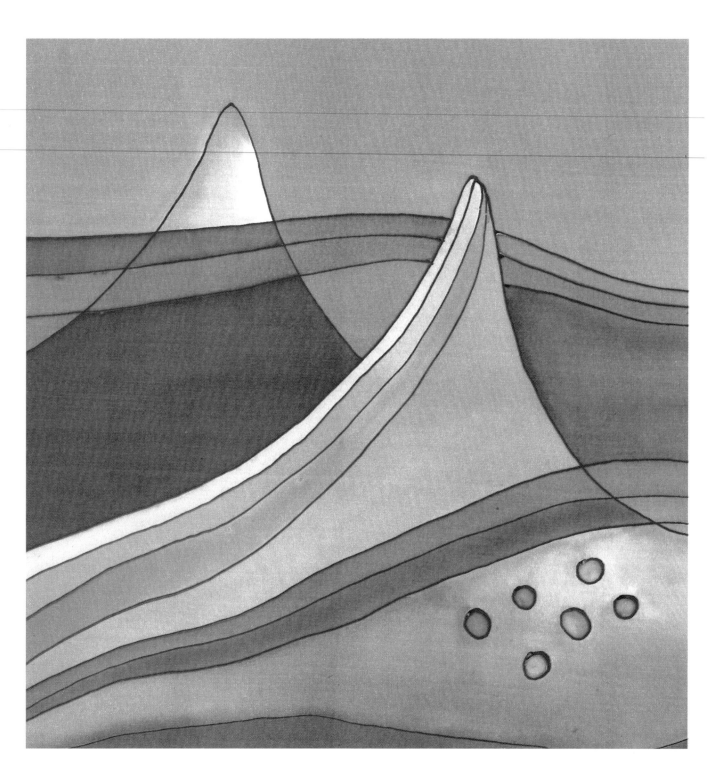

Examples

These abstract mountains, in a colour scheme of green, blue and grey, were painted in an expansive manner without any restless inner structures. Tension was introduced into the painting by the light and dark, and linear and circular contrasts.

As a contrast to the natural rounded shapes of the mountains, this composition features the angular outlines of an old stone bridge. Paint was applied to silk impregnated with a wax background, and as the paint cannot run, brush marks are visible.

To achieve the mysterious effect of this scene, no complementary colour was introduced.

A hint of green on these brownish-yellow pebbles indicates the beginning of the growth of moss. The small spots were made by flicking on alcohol. In order to paint the fine structures of the plant, an application of anti-fusant was necessary.

The four main processes for the landscape painting on the opposite page, working from left to right, are as follows:-

1) A light background is applied, indicating the sky and land. The main colouring of the completed painting is already established with this background.

2) When the background is dry, the contours of the mountains are traced with transparent gutta. It is then possible to emphasize details of the land with an application of some darker colours.

3) Jagged outlines to indicate water and alcohol spots are placed in the middle distance.

4) The mountains in the background are darkened and the clouds in the sky are dampened with water, so that the paints run into each other. To balance this, rock formations are added to the foreground.

This painting, reminiscent of minerals, has been developed out of the accidental structures which appear when salt is added. When the work was completely dry, some black gutta lines were added to emphasize and supplement the outlines. As well as the light and dark contrasts, the warm brown and cold blue tones add to the colour interest of the composition.

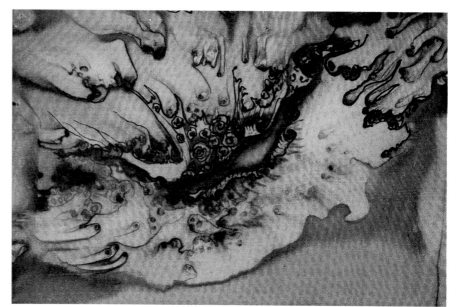

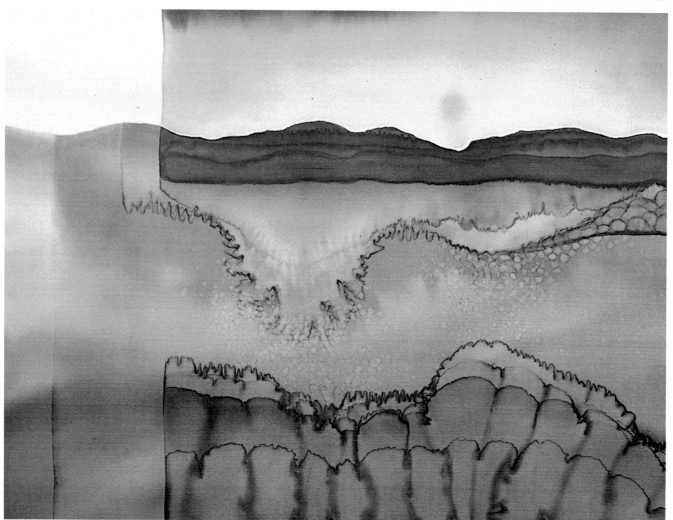

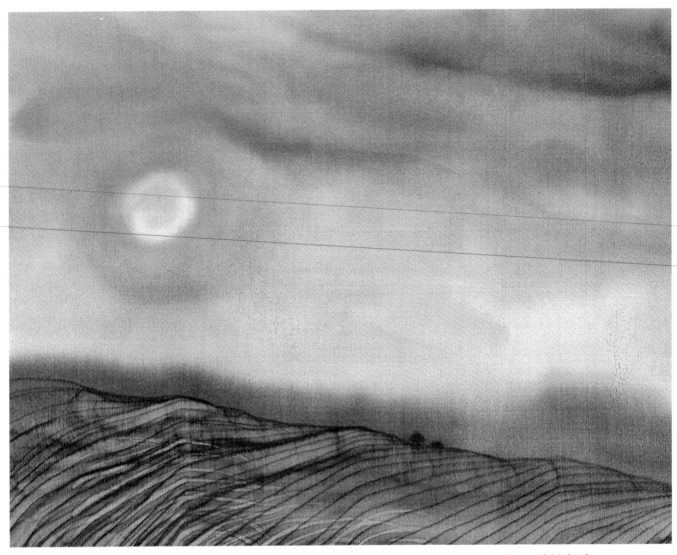

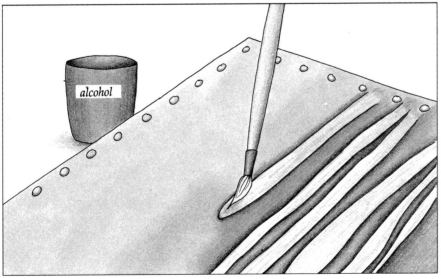

alcohol

The whole area of this landscape was dampened with water and painted with many different shades of green. In the lower part of the picture, the land is darker than the sky and the outer rim of the sun is just hinted at with pale orange. When everything was dry, the foreground area was painted with alcohol to suggest farrows. A hair dryer was used to dry the lines quickly.

This green landscape, with a castle in the background, has had alcohol lines added to the foreground. The pigments have been displaced and have reformed as dark lines. You can stop this process with a hair dryer as soon as you feel you have achieved the effect you desire.

Use has been made here of the salt effect. The resulting shapes, which resemble trees, had trunks and branches added later. Some contours were also emphasized with black gutta, to obtain more light and dark contrasts.

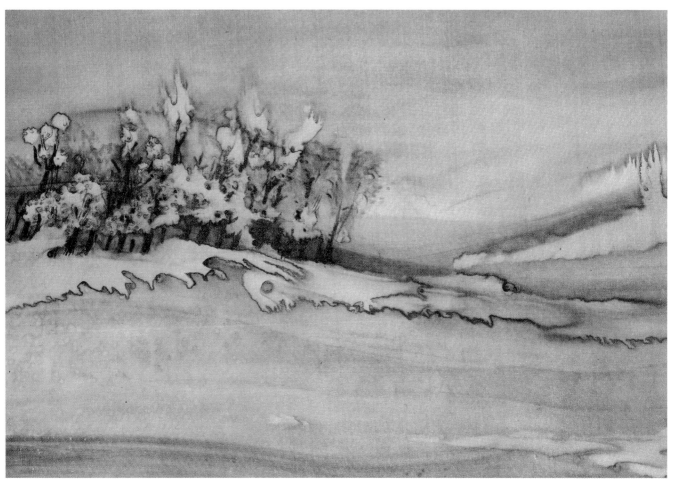

Sources of inspiration

If you look at nature with your eyes open you will become aware of the many different forms taken by rocks, stones and earth. Maybe the rounded shapes and many grey and brown shades of pebbles will inspire you, or perhaps the layered strata of rocks, such as these off the coast of Brittany.

Man-made bricks are also a product of the earth.

This desolate landscape becomes lighter towards the horizon. When translating this into a silk painting, it is best to begin with the light tones in the background, becoming stronger towards the foreground. The rocks and bushes in the foreground are the most distinct features.

A few plants among these bizarre rock
formations add colour and soften the picture.
The decayed gravestone, top right, sculpted
by man and changed by nature, creates quite
a different effect.

In the remaining illustrations a single plant
against the rock gives a strong contrast; the
wind leaves impressions on the sand and the
building materials used for the bridge and
wall blend into their surroundings.

Gallery

Marie-Luise Krutzky
Without title
38 × 38cm (15 × 15in)
Gutta and watercolour techniques on pongé

Irene E. Corts
Rocky coast
60 × 80cm (23½ × 31½in)
Gutta and watercolour techniques on pongé

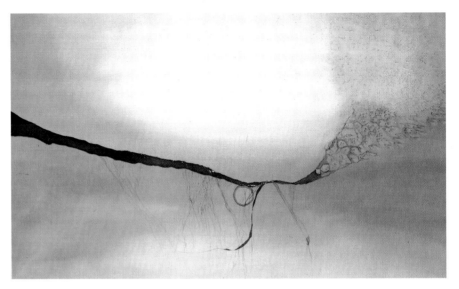

Irmes Grund
Fog by Avalon
80 × 110cm (31½ × 43¼in)
Gutta and watercolour techniques on pongé

Irmes Grund
Impressions of Sylt Island
50 × 60cm (19½ × 23½in)
Watercolour on a background
  impregnated with anti-fusant

41

Water and clouds

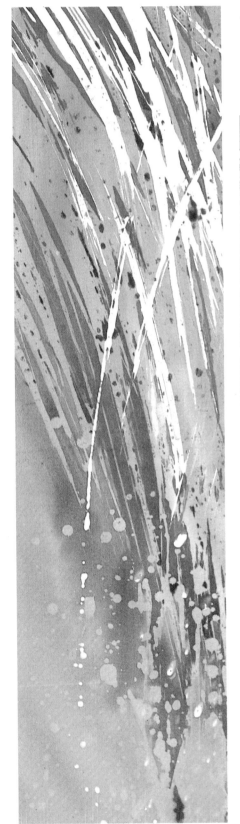

Examples

To create these swirling white lines and splashes, hot wax was applied to the unpainted silk, then the restless water patterns were painted with a broad, stiff brush. Repeated layers of wax, and tone on tone paint were then applied.

A Norwegian landscape with an interesting colour scheme of violet and green.

The strong contours were achieved with transparent gutta lines, painted on to colour-washed silk, to prevent irritating white resist lines. Begin with the gutta lines in the foreground, to create depth by overlapping some of the rock shapes. Another way to create depth, apart from the difference in size, is to apply darker tones in the foreground and lighter ones in the background.

To obtain the soft cloud edges, paint with dark colours on silk dampened with water. The paint will flow out, but will not form dark rims.

Because of the very strong light and dark contrasts in this seascape, shades of one colour family only were used. The reflections on the water, and the moon, were created with wax, then the whole background was painted over, tone on tone. After this, the rock edges were outlined with transparent gutta and the shapes darkened.

This combination of wax and gutta techniques produces calm areas with soft colour changes in the background and strong splashes of colour with sharp contours in the foreground.

The three main processes for the seascape painting shown here, working from left to right, are as follows:-

1) Dampen the silk with water before painting to achieve a soft, tone on tone foundation. For the white clouds, lift off some of the paint with alcohol.

2) Paint the mountains and foreground areas with paint diluted with alcohol. For the mountains, use a very light shade to create the illusion of depth to the background. When this is dry, paint in the middle range with stronger tones. Finally, the closest range is painted with an even stronger and slightly warmer tone. With the aid of alcohol, define the dark shore line.

3) In order to paint the fine details of the reeds, cover the whole area with a coat of anti-fusant, and allow this to dry. Don't add too much detail, or you will destroy the tranquility of the picture.

Sources of inspiration

In water and clouds, nature is forever forming and reforming structures and moods, but all of these changes do not come about by chance. They tell the careful observer a lot about the laws of nature which govern such formations. Colour and light create provocative moods, as seen in the picture on the right. Next to the dramatic glower in the sky, the calm water plays a minor role. The soft colour changes are easily reproduced with silk painting techniques and, finally, the shoreline and branches are accentuated with black gutta lines.

In contrast, the friendly blue sky below could easily be recaptured with the wax technique.

A strong light and dark contrast is created here by the white Atlantic breakers against the dark rocks. The ocean is more green than blue.

The photograph below shows a disturbed reflection in a water container.

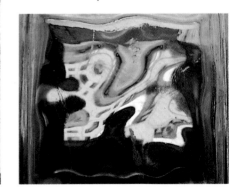

46

This picture shows a drop of sap on a cut vine in spring. We can even see part of the vineyard in the reflection.

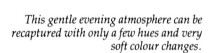

This gentle evening atmosphere can be recaptured with only a few hues and very soft colour changes.

We also see water in the shape of icicles. Their sharp edges would be created with gutta lines.

The lines of boats are seen as a colourful highlight in the otherwise dull surroundings and the unusual perspective gives added interest.

In the landscape below, the sky and water contrast starkly with the land outlines.

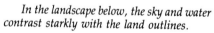

Gallery

Eva-Maria Lange
The shell
55 × 75cm (21¾ × 29½in)
Mixture of techniques on pongé

Marianne Laurent
Lake scene
25 × 30cm (9¾ × 11¾in)
Batik on satin

Brigitte Hiss
Clouds
115 × 85cm (45¼ × 33½in)
Gutta and watercolour techniques on
georgette

Marion Helbing-Mücke
Endless waters
Kimono
Crepe de chine

Trees

Trees in summer: This picture was painted on an anti-fusant background and the size of the trees is important to the impact created.

Tree in spring: Blossom and leaves were given shape by the use of alcohol spots in the crown of the tree.

Examples

Tree in autumn: The sky and earth were first painted in, then the crown of the tree was prepared with the use of salt and flicked on paint.

An anti-fusant background was then applied, to enable the very fine branches, twigs and birds to be painted without the paints spreading.

Trees in winter: Here again, the details were painted on to an anti-fusant background. After the sky had been coloured in with cool blue tones and the snow covered field indicated, the bizarre vegetation was created by blowing paint through a drinking straw over the silk.

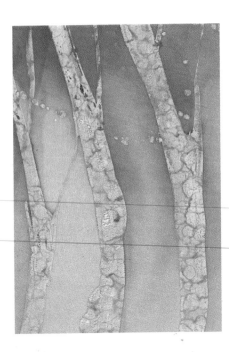

This example, left, shows the technique of painting on wax. The whole background was first covered with blue. Texture was added afterwards by flicking on alcohol.

To define the tree shapes, the trunks and a few branches were painted on to the silk with hot wax. Once the trunks had been outlined, the bark effect was achieved with alcohol shapes. Selected areas were then darkened, especially towards the top of the painting.

Right, wax was not used as a resist here but after painting the background, the outlines of the trees and branches were drawn in with gutta.

A paint and alcohol mixture was reapplied to the background and foreground and the crowns of the trees treated with salt. Then the bark was painted with a strong blue tone and textured with spots of alcohol.

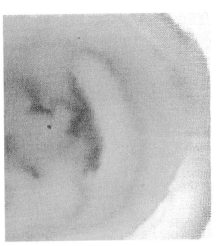

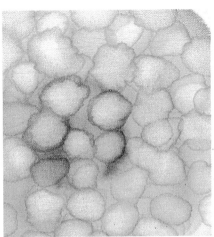

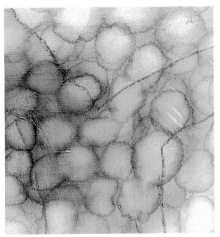

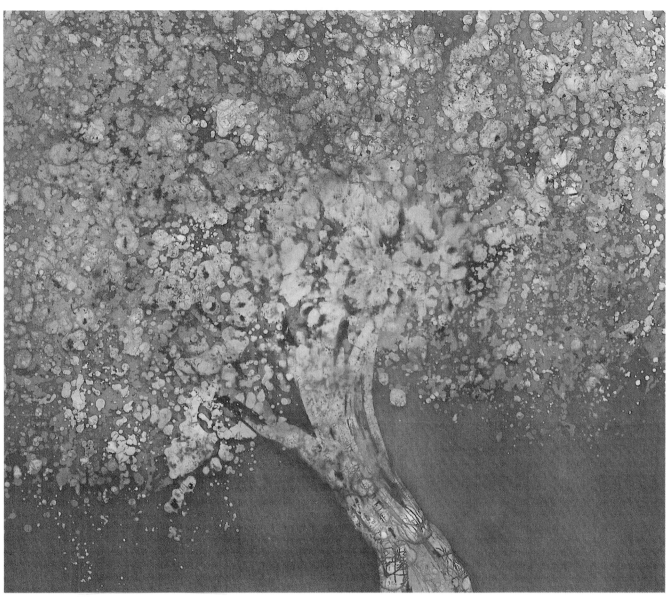

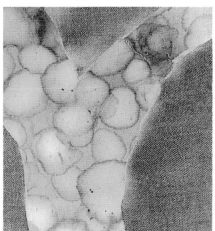

This sturdy apple tree is another example of the false batik technique. The interesting background colour was achieved by lavishly painting tone on tone, from light yellow painted over with a stronger yellow and olive green, to a blue-green. The background was then broken up with spots of alcohol.

When the painting was completely dry, the trunk of the tree was outlined with hot wax and the crown brought to life with spots of hot wax. Everything was finally overlaid with dark green. The areas covered with wax were not penetrated by the paint and after the wax had been removed, the original texture was exposed.

On the left you can see the different steps used for the false batik technique. An area is painted in a lively way, then tone on tone and further texture added with alcohol, or by other means. The shape which has to retain this texture is painted out with wax, then the rest is painted over with another colour, which will not penetrate the wax.

Don't draw trees from just one example but observe the many different silhouettes produced by nature. The same also applies to the individual leaves.

There are no extreme colour differences in this example but contrasts in light and dark, small and large, near and far, and of fine lines and restful spaces dominate this picture. The outlines were drawn with black gutta.

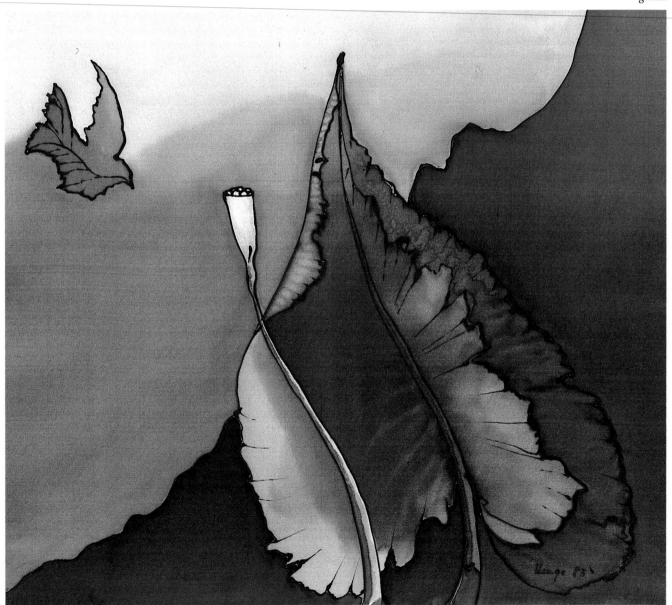

The four main stages of this scarf painted with leaves, working clockwise from the top left-hand corner, are as follows:-

1) Paint a light background and when dry, draw the outlines of the leaves and their veins with pale green gutta.

2) To give texture to the leaves, fill them in with a mixture of water and paint and add salt. The surrounding area is coloured with a darker tone.

3) Now add the remaining half hidden leaves with gutta and fill them in with paint.

4) To add more texture, after the paints have dried go over some areas of the leaves with water. Paint the background again and repeat these processes so that many layers overlap each other. After the painting has been fixed and the gutta removed, as a final touch add some glitter, noting that gold or silver gutta should be dry-cleaned.

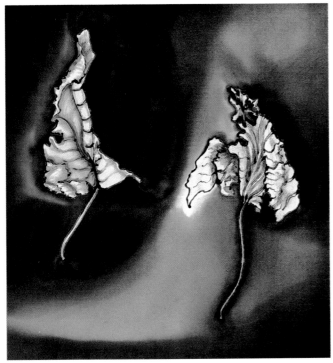

In this picture the leaves have dried out and shrivelled up, as they would in autumn. It is not always necessary to copy the colours of nature exactly and it is often more interesting to change the mood deliberately. The leaf on the right is painted in tones of brown, while the one on the left picks up the colour of the background. This gives a surrealist effect to the painting.

55

Sources of inspiration

When you decide to introduce trees into your silk paintings, it is not always necessary to show them in their full glory. Why not change your perspective and look for new angles?

Concentrate your attention on some specific detail, such as the bright red apples or pine flowers shown here. Or perhaps a stump of gnarled wood, with its interesting texture, will inspire you. On the other hand, when looking at the forest in summer don't get involved in too much detail and just accentuate the branches sparingly.

The theme of trees in the different seasons of the year has already been explored but it is sometimes tempting to add trees in a seasonal mood to a larger landscape, above.

The close-up on the right tells the viewer that it is not winter and the interest is aroused by the play of light. It makes the green and yellow of the variegated leaves shimmer in many different shades.

In this picture, the oranges show up brilliantly against the foliage, as orange and green are far apart from each other in the colour circle.

The unusual perspective and many different shades and tones of green make this picture interesting. Another point of interest is the just visible stretch of water. Its colour and calm surface contrast with the texture of the trees.

Marianne Laurent
Birches by the lake
30 × 40cm (11¾ × 15¾in)
Collage of batik, net and
feathers on pongé

Susanne Holtwiesche-Misgeld
Walk in the moon forest
58 × 100cm (22¾ × 39½in)
Collage and silk painting

Marlén Wefers
Fruit trees
45 × 68cm (17¾ × 26¾in)
Gutta, contour paints
and silk paints on pongé

59

Blossom and fruit

Examples

Leaves and flowers have been used to create the design above. The stylized leaves add weight to the corners, mostly in the bottom left-hand corner, and all the stems also begin there. This is counter-balanced by the large pink flower.

The lotus blossom scarf shown opposite was inspired by a traditional Japanese motif. The stems are extended over the dark green edge of the border.

A different interpretation of lotus blossoms can be seen on the scarf shown here. Following old Egyptian paintings, the flowers have been highly stylized to create a pattern. This effect has been further heightened by the repetition of the straight stalks as stripes in the centre and around the edges.

The relatively small amount of yellow appears very bright, because of the different intensive dark greens in the background.

This large peony is shown to its best advantage set in a geometric frame in contrasting colours, with simple corner motifs.

The design was drawn on to a white background with transparent gutta. The light and dark colour contrasts help to create the three-dimensional effect of the petals.

61

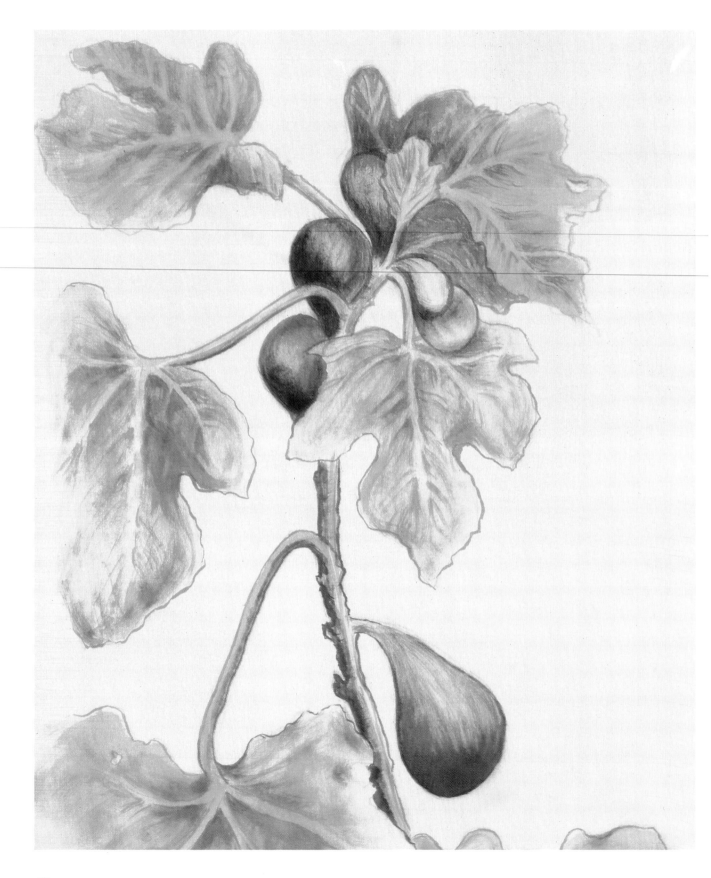

In the picture shown opposite, very fine lines have been drawn on to an anti-fusant background. The light and dark shading on the figs and leaves is easily worked with very dry paint. This creates the soft, three-dimensional effect.

Surprising results are achieved with the rubbing technique, seen in this painting of a vase and flowers.

*The silk is first impregnated with an anti-fusant solution. Arrange a few leaves and twigs on a table. Frame the silk with the **wrong** side of the silk uppermost on the frame. Now turn the frame upside down so that the silk comes into direct contact with the foliage. Wearing rubber gloves, apply some very dry paint with cotton wool to what is now the right side of the silk, so that you show up the shapes of the foliage. When the rubbing is completed, more detail can be added in the usual way.*

In these two rubbing experiments, the leaf was arranged with its underside uppermost. The twig gives the impression of movement, as its position was changed several times during rubbing.

A strong impregnation with a salt solution caused the coral-like texture in the background of this painting. The colour scheme makes use of strong contrasts, with the primary colours red, blue and yellow set against greens and browns.

A blossom can be painted in a naturalistic way or, as shown here, just by giving an impression with stylized and simplified outlines of the petal arrangement.

To achieve this effect, first draw the motif with transparent gutta, beginning in the centre and linking irregularly shaped semicircles together. In addition, the edges of the petals should curl towards the middle. Now draw in the outlines of the spiky leaves surrounding the blossom.

To create shadowy colour changes, parts of the dark areas of the bloom are painted, while others are brushed with an alcohol-water mixture and the join is immediately rubbed with a stiff, dry brush. Add some salt to the brown-green areas of the leaves. Paint the centre of the bloom in a dark shade and texture it with some alcohol spots. Finally, fill in the background with a dark colour.

Poppies as a motif are very popular and in the example shown here the flower heads are represented quite realistically, whilst the stems are arranged as a pattern.

The strong contrast of the red and green against the black is very effective, and the red of the flowers is also used for the striped and checked border pattern. The soft wavy lines of the poppies and the stark geometric forms of the border pattern also make an interesting contrast.

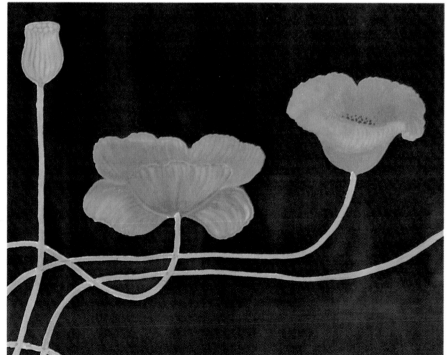

The background was coloured to start with, so the lines drawn with transparent gutta are not visible. The delicate petals of the poppies have been lightened in areas with alcohol.

The four flowers each show a separate stage, from bud to fully opened flower. This composition looks more natural than when all four blooms are at the same stage of development.

65

Sources of inspiration

Nature seems to have thought up a
multitude of different combinations of
shapes, colours and textures for fruits and
flowers and silk painting is particularly
suited to re-creating this wealth of design
ideas.

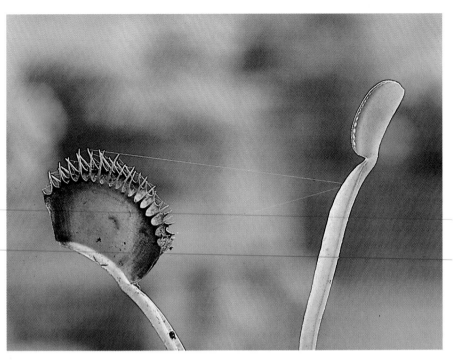

Don't limit your ideas to just the colourful
creations, left, but try something with an
unusual appeal, such as the meat eating
plant, right.

The rather fussy flower heads on the left call
for a completely different technique to the
toadstools shown below.

The texture of firm, full fruit can vary from rough, smooth, shiny or dull to speckled. Pay particular attention to light and shadow, as well as the different colour tones and surface texture.

It is better to give an impression of a mass of flowers, without too much detail.

In your search for motifs, try looking in the kitchen! The photo above shows a piece of onion skin and this layered pattern could easily be reproduced with paints and alcohol. In this way you can create colour displacements and concentrations.

The red flower is pushed into the foreground by the complementary colour, green. The background has also been toned down with other colours to underline the effect.

Gallery

Irene E. Corts
Water-lily
23 × 28cm (9 × 11in)
Gutta technique on crepe de chine

Irene E. Corts
Water-wagtail on a lotus leaf
33 × 42cm (13 × 16½in)
Watercolour on pongé

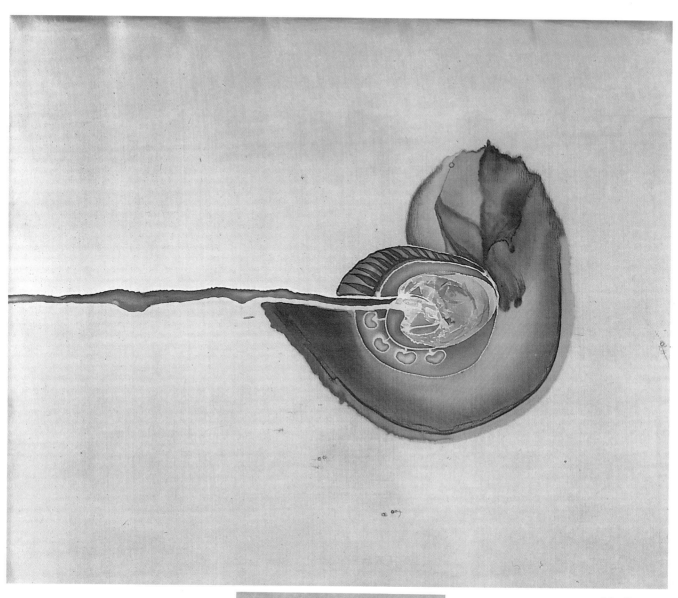

Monika Nelles
Fruit with protecting shell
59 × 84cm (23 × 33in)
Painted silk padded with foam

Marlén Wefers
Scarf
90 × 90cm (35½ × 35½in)

Animals

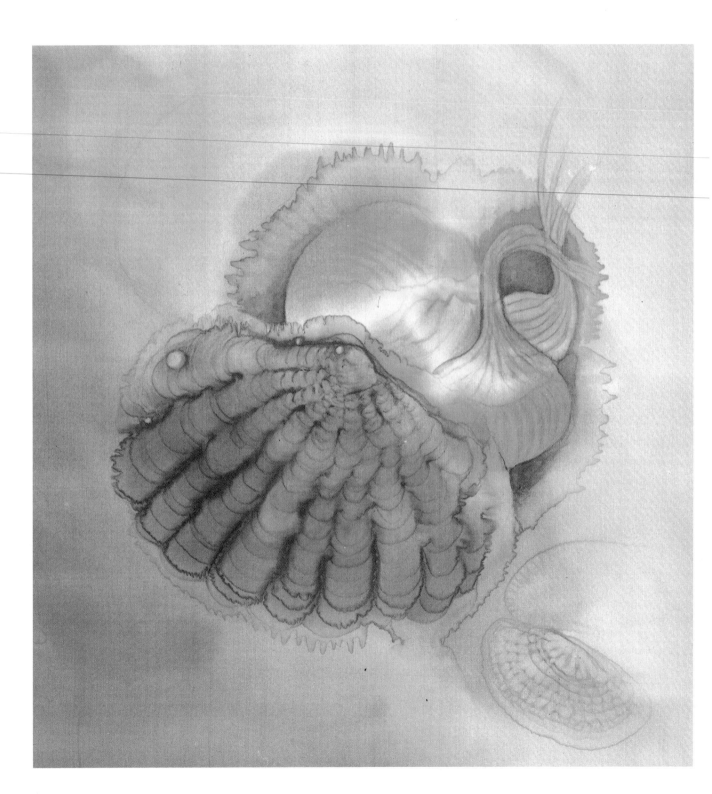

These sketches illustrate that shape as well as pattern can be varied. The scales play a part in the design.

In contrast to the colourful cockerel opposite, this abstract bird theme is a composition in blue. Many different tones have been used and the complementary greens and violets add tension.

Again, the birds have been stylized and decorated with patterns but the background is also patterned. The two strong shapes on the right counter-balance the heads. They also repeat the design of the 'eye' in the peacock's tail, thus underlining its importance.

This delightful flying bird is the work of a child of eight. The outlines were drawn with gutta and then coloured in but the colour sequence on the body of the bird is particularly imaginative. The colours appear very brilliant because of the black background.

73

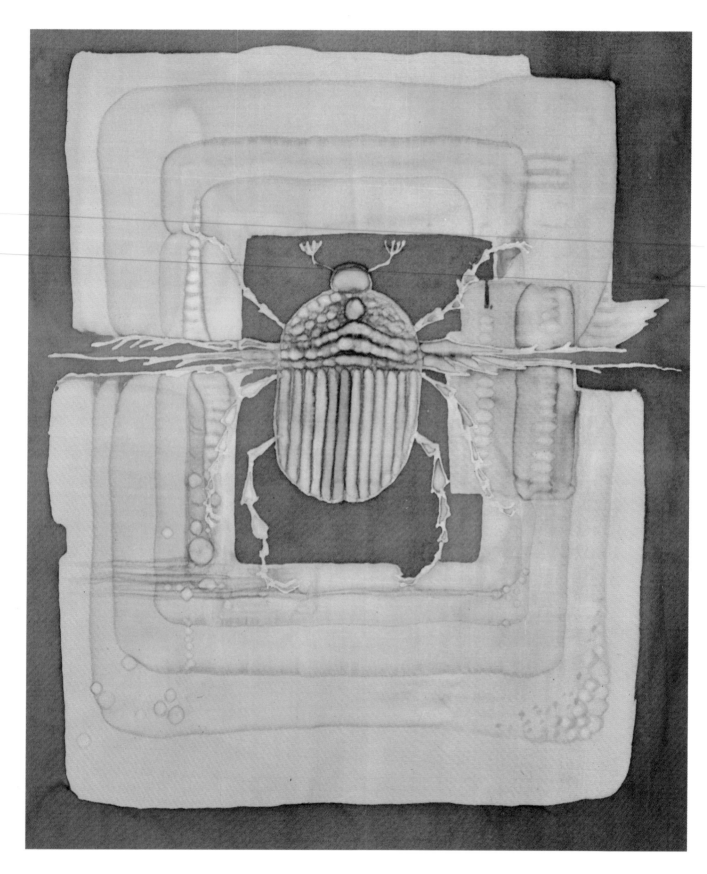

This beetle, imprisoned in blue-green tones, was drawn with gutta on to a light green background, which was then covered with toning rectangles of diminishing size. The beetle then had parallel lines and spots added with alcohol.

To bring the whole composition together, this design element was repeated several times on the background, creating a feeling of nature united with fantasy.

These two beautiful butterflies owe their liveliness to the accidental patterns which are created when salt is applied to wet paint. Using this method the different colours in the wings don't have any definite outlines.

The design on the right was painted on a light background and the spreading of the paint formed jagged outlines. In the picture below, gutta lines were added after the paint had spread and the dark wing tips were painted in.

Draw the body outline and the shape of four wings and the antenna with gutta. If you prefer you can connect the outlines of the four wings. Begin to apply colour from the centre and then add some salt. The paints will then spread outwards in a jagged line. Further decoration can be added later.

75

Sources of inspiration

Whether you want to depict animals in a naturalistic or stylized fashion, singly or in groups, or just one aspect of their appearance, always try and capture them in their natural habitat. Each one of the same species has a different body shape, colour and pattern, also texture of fur, skin, scales or feathers.

This imposing male mandrill shows a strong contrast between his soft fur and the well-defined shapes of his colourful features.

The fur of the jaguar, on the other hand, shows a random, all-over spotted pattern.

These king penguins show clear colour changes while the moth has soft colour blending.

For a change, concentrate your attention on just one detail. The 'eye' of a peacock's tail feather is a popular motif.

These two scaly heads, seen in close-up, have texture and colour appeal.

The under water world has an especial charm, as this view of coral illustrates.

The bands of colour on these fishes are sometimes clearly defined and at others the colours run into each other – the perfect subject for silk painting!

Gallery

Marianne Laurent
Summer
14 × 19cm (5½ × 7½in)
Marbling on crepe de chine

Monika Nelles **Meditation**
90 × 200cm (35½ × 79in) Painted silk and ribbons

Monika Nelles
Steadfast
42 × 59cm (16½ × 23in)
Silk with attached linen threads

Paola Incze
Two shells
80 × 90cm (31½ × 35½)
Gutta and watercolour technique

First published in Great Britain 1990
Search Press Limited
Wellwood, North Farm Road,
Tunbridge Wells, Kent TN2 3DR

in association with

Max A. Harrell
P.O. Box 92
Burnley
Victoria 3121
Australia

English translation copyright © Search Press Ltd 1990

Originally published in Germany by Falken-Verlag GmbH, 6272
Niedernhausen/TS copyright © 1988

The following artists have made their work available for the "Gallery" sections in this book:
Irene E. Corts, Irmes Grund, Marie-Luise Krutzky, Eva-Maria Lange, Marianne Laurent,
Brigitte Hiss, Susanne Holtwiesche-Misgeld, Monika Nelles, Marlen Wefers, Marion
Helbing-Mucke, Paola Incze.

Translated by Gisela Banbury
Drawings by Ulrike Hoffman

Photographs and paintings: Toni Angermayer: page 76 top left; right; bottom left; page 77 top
left; bottom left. Sigi Köster: page 77 bottom right. Henry Blanke: page 38 upper right; page 39
bottom left; page 46 bottom left; page 47 top left; middle right; bottom left; page 56 top right;
page 57 top right; page 66 bottom right; page 67 bottom left. Regine Felsch: page 20 top left;
page 39 top right; page 56 top left; page 66 top right; page 67 bottom right. Gerhard Burock:
pages 1, 2, 4, 6, 8, 10, 13, 15–18, 20, 23, 26, 27 left, top; 28 left; 29 bottom; 30–37, 42–45, 48 top;
50–55, 60–65, 70–75, 79. Irene Corts: page 40 bottom; 68. Irmes Grund: page 41. Marion
Helbing-Mucke: page 49 bottom. Brigitte Hiss: page 49 top. Susanne Holtwiesche-Misgeld:
page 59 top. Marie-Luise Krutzky: page 40 top. Marianne Laurent: page 48 bottom; 58. Erhard
Müller: page 8; page 20 bottom right; bottom left; top left; 25; 27 left, bottom; 28 right; 29 top;
38 top left, bottom left, bottom right; 39 top left, centre right, bottom right; 46 top right, top
left, bottom right; 47 top right, bottom right; 56 bottom; 57 top left, bottom; 66 top left; 67 top
right, top left. Assad Shoufany: page 69 top; 78 right; 79 left. Reinhard-Tierfoto: page 76
bottom right; 77 top right. Marlen Wefers: page 59 bottom; 69 bottom. Front cover: painting
Gerhard Burock, photograph Erhard Müller. Back cover: photographs Erhard Müller.

ISBN 0 85532 678 6

Composition by Genesis Typesetting, Laser Quay, Rochester, Kent
Printed in Singapore